The TRAILS of AMBEDKAR

ABHINAV

First Published in April 2023

ISBN: 978-93-5741-584-2

BLUEROSE PUBLISHERS
www.BlueRoseONE.com
info@bluerosepublishers.com
+91 8882 898 898

Cover Design:
Muskan Sachdeva

Cover Illustration:
Pooja Bishnoi

Typographic Design:
Pooja Sharma

Distributed by: BlueRose, Amazon, Flipkart

Dedicated to Bharat Ratna Babasaheb Dr. B. R. Ambedkar, who always fought for millions of people suffering from the discrimination of arbitrary social institutions.

The Trails Of Ambedkar

Abhinav is an ardent author, and currently a research scholar at the University of Delhi. He likes to illustrate social problems including caste, race, gender, poverty, and discrimination in fiction.

His ability to simplify complicated ideas makes his writing accessible to a wide audience, and he has always wanted to start meaningful debates about important issues. His debut book "Ambedkar and his trails" shows his profound dedication to social justice and gives unique insights into some of today's most important issues.

Forewords

---◆○◆---

As the professor of history at the department of African Studies, Faculty of Social Sciences, University of Delhi, I am glad to introduce this unique and thought-provoking book, "The Trails of Ambedkar." The author's use of poetry to highlight contemporary social issues, particularly those related to caste, race, gender, and discrimination, offers readers a fresh and unique perspective. The inclusion of Ambedkar's life and ideas, along with analysis of his contemporaries, add depth and richness to this collection of poems. I recommend this book to anyone interested in social justice and the power of literature to illuminate the wisdom of Babasaheb Ambedkar. I appeal to the readers to further read the volumes of Babasaheb for more comprehensive knowledge of his thoughts.

-   Prof. Gajendra Singh

Department of African Studies,

Faculty of Social Sciences

University of Delhi, 110007.

Ambedkar is the most influential figure not just in India but in the world. He was one of the most intellectual and grand personalities of his time. The writings of Babasaheb are evidence of his exceptional intelligence and unwavering dedication to social justice. His writings cover a broad area of subjects, ranging from political philosophy to governance, political economy to religion, and societal improvement. The concepts that Ambedkar proposed regarding equality, social justice, women's rights, and above all the Constitution of India continue to have a significant impact in modern India. It is my pleasure to write for this remarkable collection of poems dedicated to Babasaheb Ambedkar. This collection of poems provides a new genre of Ambedkar's viewpoints and his biography. The author of this book captures the very essence of Babasaheb Ambedkar's vision and his spirit.

- Prof. Geeta Sahare

Department of Political Science

Lakshmibai college

University of Delhi, 110007.

Author's Note

Dear readers,

I am Abhinav, the author of "*The Trails of Ambedkar,*" and it is with great joy that I introduce to you this book that explores the life and legacy of one of India's most prominent social reformers, Dr. B.R. Ambedkar. I strive to have a significant impact on the world through my writing as a young writer and researcher. The world is complex, full of competing interests, power structures, and inequalities that often go unnoticed by those in positions of privilege.

Everything in this book is taken from the most authentic sources and prominent scholars, including the Writings and Speeches of Babasaheb Ambedkar vols 1-17, complied by Vasant Moon and published by the Dr. Ambedkar Foundation, Ministry of Social Justice & Empowerment, Govt. of India, 15, Janpath, New Delhi, 110001. Anyone could further access these documents from the website of the Department of Justice (Ministry of Law and Justice, Government of India), https://doj.gov.in/dr-b-r-ambedkar/. I have just shaped all the arguments and ideas of Ambedkar into the genre of poetry. My writing style is a fusion of academic and creative, blending together to create a unique voice that speaks to both the mind and the heart. Drawing on my experiences as a research scholar and my own personal background, I knit together intricate stories that reveal the complexities of our world.

I believe that poetry has the power to change the world. By shining a light on these issues and challenging the status quo, I hope to inspire meaningful debate and action towards creating a more just and equitable society. At the same time, I also recognise the limitations of words and acknowledge that real change can only come through collective action, cooperation, and collaboration.

As an Indian, I have always been fascinated by the complexities and contradictions of my country's social, cultural, economic, and political landscape. Despite India's progress and achievements, we continue to grapple with issues of inequality, discrimination, and injustice. Dr. Ambedkar's life and work embody the struggle for social justice and equality, and his legacy continues to inspire generations of Indians to fight against oppression and marginalisation. Writing this book has been a deeply personal journey for me, as I have explored my own identity and beliefs through the lens of social justice. I want my readers to come away from "The Trails of Ambedkar" feeling inspired and empowered to create positive change in the world. I hope that my words will serve as a catalyst for meaningful action, whether it be through personal reflection, community organising, or political advocacy.

At last, I would like to express my hurtful gratitude to all the people who have supported me in this journey, including my family, teachers, friends, as well as the scholars, whose insights and perspectives have enriched this book.

Educate, Agitate, Organise.

The next case is equally illuminating. It is a case of an Untouchable school teacher in a village in Kathiawar and is reported in the following letter which appeared in the 'Young India' a journal published by Mr. Gandhi in its issue of 12th December 1929. It expresses the difficulties he had expressed in persuading a Hindu doctor to attend to his wife who had just delivered and how the wife and child died for want of medical attention. The letter says :

"On the 5th of this month a child was born to me. On the 7th, she fell ill and suffered from loose stools. Her vitality seemed to ebb away, and her chest became inflamed. Her breathing became difficult and there was acute pain in the ribs. I went to call a doctor- but he said he would not go to the house of a Harijan, nor was he prepared to examine the child. Then I went to Nagarseth and Garasia Darbar and pleaded them to help me. The Nagarseth stood surety to the doctor for my paying his fee of two rupees. Then the doctor came but on condition that he would examine them only outside the Harijan colony. I took my wife out of the colony along with her newly born child. Then the doctor gave his thermometer to a Muslim, he gave it to me, and I gave it to my wife and then returned it by the same process after it had been applied. It was about eight o'clock in the evening and the doctor on looking at the thermometer in the light of a lamp said that the patient was suffering from pneumonia. Then the doctor went away and sent the medicine. I brought some linseed from the bazar and used it on the patient. The doctor refused to see her later, although I gave the two rupees fee. The disease is dangerous, and God alone will help us. The lamp of my life has died out.

She passed away at about two o'clock this afternoon."

The name of the Untouchable school teacher is not given. So also, the name of the doctor is not mentioned. This was at the request of the Untouchable teacher who feared reprisals. The facts are indisputable.

No explanation is necessary. The doctor, who in spite of being educated refused to apply the thermometer and treat an ailing woman in a critical condition. As a result of his refusal to treat her, the woman died. He felt no qualms of conscience in setting aside the code of conduct which is binding on his profession. The Hindu would prefer to be inhuman rather than touch an Untouchable."

- Waiting for a Visa by Dr. B. R. Ambedkar

Source: Dr. Babasaheb Ambedkar: Writings and Speeches, Vol. 12, edited by Vasant Moon (Bombay: Education Department, Government of Maharashtra, 1993), p. 687.

"Here are some of the reminiscences drawn by Dr. Ambedkar in his own handwriting. The MSS traced in the collection of the People's Education Society were published by the society as a booklet on 19th March 1990— ed."

Contents

Infant In Hamlet

In a small village in Maharashtra state,
An infant was born with a destined fate,
Born into caste oppression and societal disdain,
But his spirit refused to let him be restrained.
From a young age, he faced discrimination,
as he was scorned and considered with indignation.
His family's depressed caste, a yoke he carried,
A severe burden like others, which could him buried.

In his formative years, obstacles he faced,
Denied education, opportunities erased.
Yet his tenacity and grit prevailed.
Through struggles and hardships, he sailed.
Denied water and left thirsty and forlorn,
He had to rely on a peon.
This experience etched in his mind,
Ignited his passion, his drive to find.

Born into pain, a heart full of zeal,
Ambedkar knew the struggle for rights was real.
With perseverance and courage, he faced every trial,
His determination was unwavering all the while.
He turned his hardships into a driving force,
Fighting for justice, his passion, an unending source.
With the pain of his past, he transformed into power,
A star for the depressed, and his legacy is forever.

His voyage from a tiny village to the global stage,
Is a tribute to his bravery, an act of ultimate outrage.
Against a system that sought to hold him down,
But he roared up and wore his crown.
In his youth, he faced a tough fight,
But he stood strong and chose to ignite.
A passion for justice and equality,
a legacy that's now his reality.

Let's not forget his early years,
and the struggles he faced with murky tears.
Let's carry his message with us today,
and work towards a better world in every way.
His spirit lives on in our hearts,
a guiding light that never departs.

Parental Vow Of Love

In the modest community of "Mhow,"
A father and son shared a bond, a vow,
To overpower the barriers of caste,
and rise together to prominence at last.
Ambedkar's father was an army man.
A learned teacher raised him.

"Ramji Maloji Sakpal" was his name.
To educate his son and break down the chains,
Of the caste system's tyrannical remnants
He instilled in him a passion for learning,
a desire that would keep his core burning,
Through the gloomiest days and the sturdiest trials,
As he pursued his dreams,
And dared the systems that denied.

Ambedkar's father died when he was young,
A loss that left him feeling lonesome and unsung.
He carried his father's wisdom in his heart,
and used them as a track to chart the parts of treasured art.
His father's wisdom was not just academic,
But moral and ethical, a plan for a life that's energetic.
He skilled him with the values of equality and honest,
and to stand up for what's right, no matter the cost.

Mother, called Bhimabai, was a woman of strength,
A pillar of support who went to excellent lengths,
To confirm that her son received an education,
and that he was not carried back by social oppression.
Because she saw the importance of learning.
She even worked hard to provide for her family, yearning,
For a better life for her son and her daughter,
in a cruel realm that often treated them like fodder.
She poured into him a wisdom of worth.
A trust in himself and his own birth,
As a human being with rights and dignity,
A faith that he would carry throughout with certainty.

He recognised that his parents would be proud,
Of the man he had become, and the fights he vowed,
To fight for the rights of the depressed,
And to challenge the system that bound them repressed.
As he rose up in the world to the peak echelons of power,
He never forgot his parents' trails of light every single hour.
He used their standpoint to fight for the browbeaten,
And to bring the alteration to a realm that's often forgotten.

Ambedkar and his parents shared a bond.
A love that transcended caste and went beyond,
a bond that enthused a spirit of hope,
and a dream of a world that's inclusive in scope.
As we rejoice in his works and his legacy,
Let us reminisce about the tie he shared with his family.
And let us convey his parents' wisdom in our hearts,
And use them to chaperone us as we play our part.

With strength and courage in their hearts,
Ambedkar and his family played their parts,
Fighting against societal woes,
to find a path where justice flows.
Through struggles and hardships, they fought,
Their spirit was unbroken, their determination wrought,
A story of hope and inspiration,
for those facing discrimination and oppression.

Partners In Passionate Struggle

—◦—

Behind every great man stands,

a strong and caring woman, one who understands.

In Byculla's open shed, a marriage was sanctified,

With a girl of just nine, Ambedkar became tied.

"Rami," renamed Ramabai, became his lifelong mate.

Their wedding may seem odd, but love knows no fate.

Ramabai, Ambedkar's soulmate true,

With courage and faith, she saw him through.

In all his tribulations, she did not hesitate.

Her unwavering support; strength; mate

Through thick and thin, she stood by his side.

In times of darkness, she remained his guide.

a foundation firm, unbreakable,

Their love and bond are unshakable.

Hand in hand, through hardships and pain,
Together, they faced society's disdain,
From the caste system's oppression,
To society's ugly juggle, their mission.
Working as a team, standing tall,
To fight for justice and equality for all,
For the Indian dream, they laboured hard,
Their love and dedication never marred.

Ramabai was illiterate yet skilled,
shared Ambedkar's vision, their fate,
Standing by him as a human being,
For the upliftment of the downtrodden, seeing.
Their passion, conviction, unbroken,
As they worked hard, with words spoken,
To bring about change and make a difference,
Their love and partnership formed an alliance.

In 1935, a loss made him break,
His wife, Ramabai, departed from his life,
A personal setback that made his heart ache,
But he kept widowhood, avoiding strife.
Thirteen years without a spouse by his side,
Ambedkar continued to fight for what's right,
His love story may not be grand or bright,
But his devotion to the cause was a shining light.

Together, they embarked on a journey,

To eradicate the oppressive attorney,

To uplift the depressed and create a new India,

Where caste and discrimination were mere insignia.

We remember Ambedkar and his wife Ramabai,

A partnership of love & struggle that will never die,

They fought for a cause that was greater than themselves.

liberation of humanity from all oppressive shelves.

Partners In Social Justice

✦

Ambedkar, a name that needs no introduction,

Always fought for social justice and inspired a revolution,

In his quest to eradicate caste and fight for equality,

He found a partner in "Sharda Kabir," a woman of nobility.

Later became "Savita Ambedkar," a woman of intelligence.

She fought for women's rights with all her resilience.

Met Ambedkar, with a shared vision to create a better world,

A world where all were equal, and all were heard.

From humble beginnings in Bombay, she came,

A bright and determined girl with a dream to aim,

She studied hard and achieved her MBBS degree,

becoming a medical officer, a pioneer, for all to see.

Sharada Kabir, a name with promise and pride,

A woman who broke barriers and defied the tide,

On April 15, 1948, she married Babasaheb Ambedkar.

And Savita Ambedkar became her name thereafter.

She paved the way for many with her first-class role,

a symbol of hope and a beacon for the whole.

In union with Babasaheb, Savita found,

A life of service, devotion to abound,

Her care for him was unwavering till the end.

His health was her priority, and her heart was blended.

Together they embraced Buddhism's way,

On Ashok Vijaya Dashami's holy day,

In Deeksha Bhoomi, Nagpur, they did vow,

To follow Buddha's path and his teachings avow.

When Babasaheb was bestowed with the highest acclaim,

The Bharat Ratna, Savita, accepted it with grace.

Honoured by the President, her love for him is untamed.

a partner, by his side till the end of his race.

Together, they fought for the rights of women,

A group that was doubly depressed, by caste and by men,

They worked to educate and empower women of all castes.

to fight for their rights and break free from society's biases.

Knowledge is power, Savita believed,

Education can change all that's perceived,

The opportunities she created for women to grow.

Breaking the chains and letting their potential show.

They worked hard for a noble aim.

Fighting for rights without any shame,

Caste annihilation was their mission,

And for women, they fought with conviction.

Ambedkar and Savita fought for a shared dream,

To break free from caste and gender, it may seem,

Their partnership was one of respect and trust.

A better society, they built, in which all are just.

Babasaheb and Savita Ambedkar,

Together they fought harder,

For a world without oppression,

Their legacy is an inspiring lesson.

Their partnership is a guiding light,

Toward a future, that's truly bright,

Breaking down barriers, they worked hand in hand,

A better world is their ultimate demand.

Tranquillity Of Salvation

Amidst the tranquil estate of the University of Mumbai,

young Ambedkar began his journey, with ambitions high.

The first member of his untouchable community,

To pursue higher education with unswerving dignity.

The struggles he encountered were immense.

As discrimination and prejudice saw him with no defence,

But he persisted, with his razor-sharp mind,

Ultimately, he became a beacon of hope for his kind.

Ambedkar, a young man hungry for knowledge,

found himself in 1908 at Elphinstone College,

It was an institution of higher learning,

With a history of brilliance and a passion for yearning,

Elphinstone College was a steppingstone,

A foundation for his future, a place to hone,

A place where the best and the brightest would go,

To learn, to gain, to grow, and to sow.

But for Ambedkar, it was not all roses and sunshine.
For he faced Casteism, common trouble at that time,
From his peers and professors, who saw him as unique,
And held onto their caste with a conviction that was ardent.
But he would not be daunted, would not back down.
He studied hard and defied the status quo with a frown.
He shone in his studies and earned many accolades.
Shattering the glass ceilings that blockade.

As he dove deeper into his studies,
He got that education was crucial,
to be free from the caste-bound shambles.
With his exceptional academic accomplishments,
He inspired several to pursue their aspirations,
and achieve life's fulfilments.
In the university, he discovered his voice,
a stand to challenge the system and make a choice.
His paper on the "caste system," an innovative work,
opened the murky senses and led to a societal perk.

He turned to education in the United States,
Where he earned expertise that he would later translate,
into policies that would outline the future of his nation,
And pave the way for a better society, a new foundation.
Ambedkar's life in university was not without discord,
as he faced injustice, discrimination, and huge bias.
But with his unswerving spirit and determination,
helped him seize these hurdles and achieve great elevation.

He became an inspiration of faith for the subjugated.
A winner of social justice, and a symbol well educated.
His voyages to the university may have halted long ago,
But his impact and influence persist and grow.
As we commemorate his life and his contributions,
Let's learn the lessons he taught and pursue new solutions.

To the disputes and challenges that persist,
And continue to work for a world that's brighter and just.
During Ambedkar's life at the university,
Was not just a personal journey but a song of unity.
A melody to break down the walls of division,
And to build a society that's purely based on inclusion.

Academic Odyssey For Liberation

Ambedkar's journey took him far and wide,

From India to London and beneath the tide,

To Columbia University, a place of great fame,

where he sought to broaden his intellectual base.

At LSE, he studied economics and law,

And honed his skills with great foresight,

But at Columbia, he broadened his horizons,

And in sociology, he found his passion.

The year was 1913, a time of great change,

in an India that was still struggling to rearrange.

In Columbia, he found a new sense of purpose,

As he dove into the study of social justice.

He saw the inequalities that dogged his native home,

And with new ideas, he knew he must roam.

In Columbia, Ambedkar faced prejudice and pain,

But he persevered and earned his Ph.D. with great gain,

Back in India, he returned with a mission,

To end the caste system and break free from oppression.

His journey continued at the London School of Economics,

Where he honed his skills in law with great ethics,

Gray's Inn welcomed him with open arms,

A new chapter in his life, full of great charms.

Unquenched Thirst

<hr>

In Bombay's land of governance and power,
A directive was issued in a resolution's hour,
To grant civil rights to the depressed classes,
But many boards and municipalities were shameless.
Mahad Municipality was among those who denied,
Ignoring the resolution with malice and pride.

The Bombay Legislative Council passed another resolution,
To deny financial grants for this gross persecution.
Finally, the Maher Municipality opened the tank,
Known for its delicious water and social rank,
Ambedkar organized the Dalits to assert their rights,
To drink and take water from the tank in sight.
Thousands of untouchables gathered to convene,
a historic moment, a struggle to be seen.

In the town of "Mahad," in the native lands of the Mahar,

Ambedkar manoeuvred a movement that traced very far,

To splinter the shackles of caste and to avow their rights,

To drink from the same tank and to end the incessant fights.

The Mahad Satyagraha wasn't an encounter with water,

Rather than demand parity, a decent share of what matters,

For years, depressed had been denied their equitable place,

Their thirst was unquenched, their spirits were disgraced.

Ambedkar and his admirers would not be muzzled,

They strode to the tank, their hearts undeterred,

And they sipped from it, an emblematic act of defiance,

That wobbled the stones of the caste system and its reliance.

Ambedkar said that water was only a pretext,

A means to an edge, a fight against a system that vexes,

Denied basic rights, despite their plight,

Caste should not determine a human's right.

The Mahad Satyagraha was a cornerstone in the struggle,

A juncture of valour and of spirit that would juggle,

The power dynamics of caste and question its hold,

on the hearts and minds of the depressed, young, and old.

For Ambedkar and his admirers, it was a song to arms,

A souvenir that they had agency and the ability to disarm.

The depressive systems of society, and to reclaim,

Their dignity, and their abide spaces in the game.

We proudly remember the Satyagraha and its mentor,

A man of sight, of courage, and of persistent temper,

He dared to enter a world beyond caste's memory,

Where justice and equality were the ultimate key.

Divine Doors Open: A Symbol Of Inclusion

In Old Nashik stands Kala Ram Temple grand,
Built long ago by Sardar Odhekar's hand,
Thousands come for blessings from Lord Ram,
But no Dalit or untouchable could cram.
The caste system was rigid and cruel.
prevents them from entering, a vile rule,
Practiced since ancient times, it still reigns,
A social evil that still pains.
A temple where untouchables were not allowed,
Their entry was a crime in the eyes of the crowd.

But Ambedkar, a man of great will and might,
was determined to end this oppressive plight,
He fought for the right to enter the temple with grace.
to end the caste system's oppressive embrace.
15,000 people joined in a peaceful fight,
To enter Kala Ram Temple with their might,
Singing bhajans, they sat before its gates,
But the police and orthodox Hindus met them with hate.

The untouchables faced harsh treatment too.
Their kids were expelled, roads closed, and shopping taboo,
Despite this provocation, Ambedkar showed restraint.
and kept his Satyagrahis from acting with the complaint.
The temple authorities and the upper caste
were outraged at Ambedkar's act,
They tried to stop him, to block his path,
But he persevered, with courage and steadfast.

For five years, the Satyagrahis stood their ground,
15,000 strong, for equal rights they found,
The Kala Ram temple, a symbol of the caste divide,
They excluded the untouchables, but they didn't hide.
Finally, the temple gates opened to all,
The untouchables' heads held high, no longer to fall.

Ambedkar's words, "We should have rights," were the goal,
And their peaceful Satyagraha had won its role.
Ambedkar's struggle was not just for the temple,
But for the end of oppression and discrimination ample,
His fight was for the rights of every human being.
for a world where every person was seen.

His fight was a call for humanity and compassion.
In a world where caste did not dictate our actions,
His fight was a reminder of the power of the people.
to rise up and fight against oppression's steeple.
Ambedkar spoke words so clear,
His motives for temple entry were sincere,
not to worship idols or become the same,
but to end discrimination and the casteist game.

Today, we remember Ambedkar's fight,
For his courage, his will, and his might,
We remember his call for justice and piety.
for the end of the caste system's tyranny.
We remember his fight for every person's right,
To enter the temple and pray to the divine light,
We remember his message of hope and unity.
for a world where every person is free.

Echoes Of Lives That Produce Life

Amidst the dusky haze,
a gloomy truth that would always amaze,
In the history of India, a saviour stood tall,
Ambedkar, whose name resonates through the saga's hall,
He fought for the rights of the marginalized,
For the women, he never compromised.

Ambedkar realised that justice was necessary for the women,
And he took on the challenge with all his drive.
He was a brilliant scholar of law and rights,
He fought against the norms that divided society's might.
He saw the extreme need for a new legal code,
That would give every Hindu woman an equitable abode.

In India, a land of lively hues and ethnicities,
Gender inequality is a blight that still prevails.
Where women's worth is often unappreciated,
Their rights and liberties are not yet fully protected.
From birth, girls confront a world of discrimination.
Their ability is stifled by collective social expectations,
Their voices muffled by patriarchal traditions,
And their sky is limited by gendered limitations.

The Dayabhaga and Mitakshara schools of law,
They were ancient customs without a flaw.
But for Ambedkar, they were flawed.
They denied many of their legitimate rewards.
The Mitakshara gave all property to the male heir,
And the Dayabhaga gave an equivalent share.
But for women and for the depressed castes,
These customs were a prison that lasted for ages.

Western feminism, a change on the world stage,
Urging all to see beyond women's silenced rage,
But on the Indian subcontinent, friction did arise.
Social hierarchies are alien to Western eyes.
Western feminists' effects lingered, were limited,
Only reaching the elites, while many women were neglected,
Social hierarchy, a notoriously rare concept,
triggering a double burden and a cruel and unjust effect.

Indian methodologies are needed, it was clear,
To fight this vile and quell women's fear,
To address the double drawback they face,
and elevate them to their rightful place.
Ambedkar's philosophy, a stubborn attempt to think,
Considering intersectionality, a crucial link,
inclusive of gender and caste, among other things,
A holistic method to interpretation—that's what it brings.

A conjunction of casteism and sexism is crucial.
Not an insular approach but a coalesced dismissal,
of patriarchal structures, including Brahmanical,
To exterminate gender inequality, that's the goal.
Indian feminist thinkers must restrict patriarchy,
With the Indian experience for better accuracy,
To tackle the essence of the issue head-on,
and empower women until true equality is won.

Ambedkar inexorably battled for the Hindu Code Bill,
and give everyone a future that is fair enough.
The Hindu Code Bill aimed to reform,
The Hindu personal law, which was the norm,
Ambedkar always knew the bill's worth,
For it would give women their lawful berth,
He battled for it with all his might.
For he saw in it a future that was bright.

But the resistance to the bill was harsh and strong.

For patriarchy and existing norms, it had a long,

Women's rights, it endangered to upend,

And for the status quo, it did not bend.

Yet Ambedkar never quivered.

For he knew that the bill was much needed,

Ambedkar saw and examined the patriarchy's power,

How it kept women depressed, hour by hour,

Change was crucial for the nation to thrive.

And he took on the challenge with all his drive.

Patriarchy combined with casteism was a curse.

a realm that kept women in a state of worse,

It took away their voice, their rights, and their dignity.

For new India, that's called free; it was a mockery.

He saw the need for a new social order,

Where women would be free with all their honour.

For Ambedkar, the fight against patriarchy was intense.

It was a moral obligation, a mission that was a must.

For he realised that a nation's progress was tied,

to the rights of women, which were frequently denied.

For Ambedkar, patriarchy was a foe.
A force that kept women down, below,
Ambedkar's vision: it was a new dawn,
One where patriarchy would ultimately be gone,
Ambedkar's fight was a triumph.
For a nation that's free and a future that's worthwhile,
He fought for women's right to education,
For the right to work and for equal remuneration,
He saw in women a drive that was untouched.
And he fought to liberate it with all his strength.

The bill was passed, and after some time,
Even with the maximum changes, it was steep to climb,
His fight for equality never ceased.
And for the Hindu Code Bill, he gave his best,
Ambedkar's fight against the Dayabhaga and Mitakshara,
was a struggle for justice and a future that was bright.

Ambedkar truly believed in the "nature" of women.

Their strength, their resilience, and their wisdom

He knew that they had the power to lead.

to create a future that was free from greed.

Ambedkar's fight for women was not just.

into a system that was unfair and unjust,

Not for a few, but for all who were shoved,

Where their voices were silenced, their dreams burst.

He fought for the right of women to vote,

To actively participate in a system that would promote.

Equality, justice, freedom, and democracy

a system that would be free from hypocrisy.

The Hindu Code Bill, which was Ambedkar's legacy,

A law that conferred women's rights and equity,

It gave women their fair abode,

And it paved the trails for a future full of glow.

A Manifesto Of Equality

In a realm abundant with differences,

Caste has some space, if not any precedence.

But in India, it's a certainty we cannot ignore.

a system that propagates injustice at its core.

It's in this context that Ambedkar wrote,

His magnum opus, "Annihilation of Caste."

He laid bare the ills of this system so entrenched,

And exposed us to how it must be, relentlessly drenched.

For Ambedkar, the caste system was more,

Then it's just an artificial chopping of society, for sure.

It was a force that kept people depressed and down,

A system that needed to be shattered and thrown.

In "Annihilation of Caste," Ambedkar argued,

That caste was not just a matter of being relegated.

It was a force that dictated a person's destiny,

A system that destroyed individual identity.

To end the system of caste despair,
We must first admit it's there.
Reforming it is not enough,
Transformation is the true stuff.
Ambedkar fought against this curse,
which trapped his people and was perverse,
An institution of oppression so vile,
Robbing dignity with deft guile.

Ambedkar knew the cure,
To bring equality and justice, which would endure,
Caste was a disease that he had to annihilate,
So, humanity could progress and innovate.
His famous book, "Annihilation of Caste,"
A powerful message that couldn't be dispelled,
He spoke the truth and called for social reform,
A voice of change to break the caste's norm.

Ambedkar, with his vision so clear,
saw caste as a block, hindering progress and cheer,
He wanted to abolish it and end its sway,
So, the depressed could live, in a better way.
He knew caste was the cause of much discrimination,
And only its end could bring true emancipation,
He called for a social revolution, for change,
A world where all were equal, no more estranged.

A Canvas Of Rights

———◆O◆———

Babasaheb Ambedkar, the architect of the constitution,

Whose wisdom has shaped India's democratic evolution,

The Indian Constitution still exists as a testament.

To his genius and his resolute commitment.

As India's first law minister, he acted vigorously.

To make a constitution that would protect people's dignity.

He fought for the insertion of fundamental rights,

making certain that no people or citizens were left behind.

"Equality, liberty, and justice" were his path showing lights,

He realised that the nation's unity lay in its people's rights.

He knew the significance of 'freedom of speech."

And he fought for every individual to teach.

He believed in the "right to life" and "liberty,"

And he fought for the repressed, relentlessly.

His contributions to the nation cannot be measured.

His ideas and philosophies cannot be treasured.

He is the father of the Indian Constitution.

whose sight has become a national institution.

Ambedkar's contribution to the Indian Constitution
lays the groundwork for a truly democratic nation.
He stood for the poor, the beaten, and the depressed.
And fought for their rights until his last breath.
Ambedkar's work reflected a shining example,
of a man who fought for justice and equality ample.

His commitment to India's constitution-drafting,
his work as the law minister was far more extensive.
Ambedkar left an enduring mark on India's history,
His spirit of inclusion still inspires our destiny.
He fought for justice, to eliminate caste's oppression,
And his vision of equality still drives our progression.

For he saw how it had divided the nation for centuries.
Keeping people depressed and refusing basic necessities.
He worked tirelessly to create awareness,
On the importance of education and empowerment,
For he considered that knowledge and freedom
Were the keys to splitting free from the caste system.
Ambedkar's contributions were not limited to India.
His ideas and philosophies have affected the world over.

His work on fundamental rights and equality
has inspired many in their fight for their liberty.
His struggle against the caste structure and discrimination
endures inspiring people to fight for their emancipation.
Ambedkar anticipated advancement and inclusion,
Where all have an identical role in the nation's evolution.
His work on the Constitution ensures protection,
Of people's rights without any exception.

In a modern world where discrimination still exists,
And inequity on many grounds continues to persist.
Ambedkar's ideas and philosophies remain relevant.
And continue to serve as a beacon for betterment.
The "annihilation of caste" is still an objective to achieve,
For we need to end this system of oppression and relieve.
Ambedkar's contributions to India's democracy,
are enormous and continue to encourage a legacy,
For he believed in the power of the people and their rights,
And fought diligently to ensure their freedom and might.

His dedication to providing fundamental rights,
confirms that India's democracy is strong and bright.
For he knew that a nation is only as strong as its people.
And their rights and freedoms must be protected as equals.
He was a man of great vision and immense passion.
Whose legacy further inspires and keeps us in action.

Ambedkar, oh mighty warrior,

who always fought with fervour,

A crusader against inequality,

his legacy we must not disesteem.

As an elder statesman,

and national leader,

His contribution to the Constitution,

we shall forever treasure.

A champion for human rights,

and emancipator of the enslaved,

His endeavours to rid the world,

of injustice shall forever be engraved.

Rupee's Draining Pain

As a repercussion of colonial rule,

India writhed with a currency duel.

The colonisers had left their mark,

with a currency structure that was stark.

The Indian rupee was tangled to gold,

And its value was dependent on what was told,

By the Bank of England, far, far away,

Leaving India in an economically susceptible sway.

The exchange rate was frequently unfair,

And the Indian economy could barely bear,

The burden of colonial control,

on its economy and its role.

The exchange rate was a foremost flaw,

And Ambedkar saw the necessity for a law.

To normalise the value of the rupee,

And give India the power to be economically free.

The sterling exchange standard was a trap,
And Ambedkar recognised it was a handicap.
He proposed a new structure for economic gain,
And his thoughts truly relied on a game change.
British financial capitalism was a tool,
To keep India under their filthy rule.
But Ambedkar saw the necessity to break free,
And his dream gave India the major key.

The "problem of the rupee" was complex,
And Ambedkar's understandings were the apex.
His suggestions were far-reaching,
And his concepts were truly enlightening.
The Royal Commission's report was a milestone,
India's journey toward the unknown.
Ambedkar's contributions were a hallmark,
Of a man who left an ineffaceable mark.

That one man acknowledged the need for reform,
And his vision would ultimately transform,
The currency system in India's name,
To give the country a reasonable claim.
B.R. Ambedkar was his name,
A scholar with a desire and a flame,
For the rights of the people and their gain,
And the necessity for an economy to sustain.

Ambedkar realised the necessity for a central bank,

To manage the rupee and its value,

And to free India from the ranks,

Of those who held the power and authority to pursue

The Reserve Bank of India was born,

As an outcome of Ambedkar's insight,

To manage the rupee and its form,

And to give India the authority to take flight.

The central bank was the foundation stone,

Of the reforms that Ambedkar wants to make,

And with it came the power to compensate,

For the past and the improvements to undertake.

Ambedkar saw the need for a central bank,

To be independent and free from political sway,

For only then could it truly supply,

Stability is required for the economy to stay.

The RBI was the foremost of its kind,

In Asia, as a model for others to follow,

And Ambedkar's insights would unwind,

The knots of the economy's trouble and hollow.

An Epic Ode To Fairness

In a land of disparities, where prosperity and scarcity clash,

Where visions of progress often meet with a severe backlash,

Where eras of caste acumen left fathomable scars,

Reservations for the depressed were a bold step by far.

With the hand of Ambedkar, the Father of the Constitution,

The nation showed the potential for bold affirmative action,

To counter the effects of caste-based dissimilarity,

a pledge to provide to those who faced brutality.

The reservation structure in India,

A topic that often spurs debate and division,

Many believe and prejudice it to be outmoded,

An exercise that we no longer promised to abide.

But those who are breathing in the boundaries,

Those who've been depressed for centuries,

Understand that, deprived of reservation,

Equality will endure as a distant imaginary.

Ambedkar acknowledged this all too well,
He fought for the rights of the broken,
For those who were deprived of education,
And opportunities to surge up to the highest.
The caste system is still thriving well,
Despite our entitlements to modernity,
And the only way to interrupt the cycle,
Is by giving those at the end a little bit of priority.

Reservations are not a windfall,
It's a way to level the playing field,
A way to give the underprivileged,
a chance to prosper together and to yield.
It's a way to right the wrongs of the past,
And to safeguard a perkier future for all,
A way to build a sturdier, more just nation,
a nation that's proper and united, standing tall.

The significance of reservation,
cannot be rejected or ignored,
For it's the only path till now to ensure,
that justice and equality are really restored.
But many claim that it's time to look for alternatives,
A reservation has its flaws and can often be divisive,
They propose a swing to a structure based purely on merit,
Where equal opportunity is provided to all, let's hear it.

The road to such a system is troubled with challenges,
With systemic biases and societal fences to manage,
It's not likely to generate a level playing field,
By attaining true meritocracy, a decent ideal.
But perhaps the riposte lies in an amalgamation of the two,
Reservation need not be the only selection in view,
Along with it, let's provide excellent education and training,
And toil to form an inclusive society without restraining.

Let's curl a society where privilege is not based on birth,
Where all can flourish, irrespective of their worth,
Where we acclaim diversity and value individuality,
And shape a nation of equals, with unity and fraternity.
So, let's not do away with reservations in a hurry.
For it's still needed, in spaces where things are still murky,
But let's toil towards a more inclusive society,
where merit and opportunity are based on true equality.

A Path To Serenity

Ambedkar's journey, great and full of discord,
He found in Buddha's preaching, solace and soft,
A philosophy of love to end the world's strife,
To make hassles and conflicts take flight.
As a scholar and thinker, he took Buddha's voice,
And found in his preaching a new way to stride,
A path of peace, that Buddha espoused,
Became a way to end oppression and misuse.

Buddha's preaching lighted a way of grace,
A trail to equality, justice, and peace.
Ambedkar clasped it with his full faith.
Thus, the depressed found a beacon above,
Through Ambedkar, Buddha's preaching took the race,
And a new dawn of hope shone from the sky above.

Buddha told of what's not Dhamma true,

The faith in God, he said, is not due.

No supernatural soul or heavenly hue,

Dhamma's centred on alliance with what's true.

Sacrifices and erudite knowledge in vain,

The righteousness of Dhamma books hits a sturdy chain.

To discover what's genuine, let go of what's not sane,

The trail to Dhamma is an actual quest to unveil.

Discover the truth with an open mind,

Leave dogmas and illusions behind.

The path may be long and hard to find,

But the quest for Dhamma is for a peaceful mind.

Ambedkar found hope in Buddha's teachings,

Built on the foundation of justice and love, reaching.

A slope of equality, rising above,

To help the world heal and flourish, thereof.

The relevance of Buddha's teachings still holds,

To help the world with new skills, bold

Teaching that all life is sacred and pure,

Respect each other, and love shall endure.

Buddha taught that peace lies in simplicity,

To cease greed, anger, and ignorance with intensity.

Strive for compassion and tolerance,

To lead a life of spiritual sustenance.

Buddha's teachings guided a world in need,

Where peace, equality, and freedom take the lead.

Where discrimination has no place to rule,

And humanity lives in harmony as a jewel.

East-West, India Has The Best

Two people make shifts in Chronicle's Tales,
Buddha and Marx had their ideas revealed.
The middle path was Buddha's decree,
Freedom from sorrow is the trail to being free.
Marx saw society as spliced by class,
The bourgeoisie's rule he sought to surpass.
Both aimed for a society beyond the traditional range,
Buddha and Marx are constantly in change.

Two distinct paths, both aimed at change,
Buddha's and Marx's goals are so strange.
Meditation for Buddha to end desire's reign,
a stable mind, free from life's pain.
Compassion and conflict, Buddha's decree,
The cycle of life, to its end, is set free.

Marx saw a world, corrupt and vile,
and wanted to end the power of the capitalists' guile.
Both sought a world so magnificent,
Buddha brought enlightenment, an end to grief's lament.
Marx, to end the authority of the few,
and empower the masses with what is true.

Revolution was their shared ambition,
Traditional ways met their termination.
end of misery, Buddha's goal so bright,
Exploitation's end, Marx's righteous fight.
Ambedkar's visions were grand, his theories deep,
A level land, where righteousness could seep.

But to the west, he turned for a way,
Marx's notions, he found, wouldn't sway.
For Ambedkar, the issue was complex,
The caste system's hold, he sought to perplex.
Deeply seated in the people's minds,
Cracking it is a puzzle hard to unwind.

Communism's influence, in Ambedkar's time,
Promising a better world, with a radical chime.
Many were swayed by its call, but he stood his ground,
It's a lethal defect; he could never be bound.
Class-based communism failed to understand,
The caste-based subjugation is a hurdle so grand.

Its pledge to abolish class could never find,
The grip of caste held India behind.
Ambedkar denied communism in his own way.
For building his own trails, he spent his days.
His struggle was bold, his vision was pure,
His thoughts, he could not let be sold for sure.

For Ambedkar, the struggle was not just for wealth,
but for pride, respect, and mental health.
His was a brawl that would never be won,
Until caste was abolished, and justice was done.
He knew that the path he chose would be hard,
But he could not be swayed by any reward.

Ambedkar, standing steady and resolute,
Against communism's appeals, he could not repudiate.
Ambedkar realized that the answer lay,
not in communism, but in a unique way.
The challenge was not just economic,
But about social status, which is denied as demonic.

Marx spoke of the end of the bourgeoisie,
and the rise of the proletariat class, which would be free.
But Ambedkar saw a different bend.
one where the caste system would end.
He believed in the power of education,
and the annihilation of discrimination.
For he saw that the key to social change,
Lay it in the mind and the way it could be arranged.

For Ambedkar, the fight was not just about class,
But about the caste, that had to ultimately pass.
He saw that the way to end oppression.
lay in a social revolution, which was not just a confession.
And so, he stood for a different way,
one that would change society in a different way.

Ambedkar's ideas were bold and new,

And they spoke of a society that was genuine.

And though he argued with communism,

His ideas were not just about the opposition.

For he stood for the depressed, the subjugated,

And for a society that was largely uneducated.

In the end, Ambedkar's vision earned the day,

And his struggle for justice is still felt today.

He revealed to us that actual freedom is not just a dream,

But a struggle that must go on forever, it seems.

Ambedkar still lives on,

as a beacon of hope for the poor.

His vision was not just about class,

But about a civilization that was free from the caste crass.

The Voice Of The Downtrodden

"Why should I feel shy?
I have laid aside hesitation and opened my mouth.
Here, on earth, no notice is taken of a dumb creature.
No real good can be secured by over-modesty."
Tukaram (a Marathi bhakti poet)

Ambedkar and Mooknayak, a bond of fire,
Exposing liars and the caste systems' dire.
Mooknayak, a platform where voices were heard,
And the depressed were given a powerful word.
A Marathi newspaper of great renown,
Shedding light on the caste system's frown.
The hypocrisy of elites was exposed with ease,
The depressed found solace in Mooknayak's breeze.

Ambedkar, the editor, a scholar so bright,
fighting against the caste system's might.
Through Mooknayak, he spoke to the masses,
challenging norms and societal classes.
A voice of truth, cutting through oppression's chain,
Mooknayak stood with the depressed, again and again.

Ambedkar's Mooknayak was a force to reckon,
A voice for the depressed, a platform unshaken.
Challenging the caste system, questioning the norms,
Pushing the boundaries and letting the truth take its form.
A politics of assertion, Ambedkar's vision,
A new discourse on caste, a powerful conversion.
Mooknayak faced challenges, but it prevailed,
Inspiring generations, its impact never derailed.

A tool for change and resistance, a symbol of hope,
In a society unequal, where the depressed couldn't cope.
Mooknayak reminds us of the power of the written word,
to challenge, inspire, and make our voices heard.
Ambedkar's legacy, a fight against the past,
Mooknayak stands tall, a symbol that will forever last.

Vision For The Depressed

Ambedkar and Bahiskhrit Bharat, a dream to set free,
From the shackles of caste, oppression, and misery,
A call to break the walls of the caste system's design,
And pave the way for a new world where all could unite.
In 1927, Bahiskhrit Bharat was a beacon of hope,
A vision of a new world, where all could freely cope,
In a world where caste was not a barrier to one's dreams,
Where merit alone would guide the way to new extremes.

Ambedkar's call for Bahiskhrit Bharat was a cry,
For freedom from the chains that held the depressed awry,
Bahiskhrit Bharat was a vision of a new India,
Where depressed would rise with heads held high.
In a world where opportunities were not based on birth,
but on talent, hard work, and a will to unearth.
A new India where the depressed could rise,
And with their heads held high, they reach for the skies.

Ambedkar's vision was a call to break free,

From the chains of caste and to let equality be,

Bahiskhrit Bharat was hope; a new world was in sight,

A world where all can live with pride,

Where power won't belong to just the elite's side,

but with every person, old or new.

In a world where everyone could freely soar,

and the chains of caste were no more.

Crossed Paths, Shared Goals

Ambedkar and John Dewey, two minds so great,

Their paths intertwined, their work in debate,

Ambedkar from India, Dewey from the west,

Both are seeking truth in their academic quests.

In early times, they crossed ways,

Dewey, a philosopher, and Ambedkar, with a social blaze,

Their goal is to bring about change,

Break the shackles, old and strange.

For Dewey, education was the key,

To freedom and democracy for all to see,

For Ambedkar, it was the annihilation of caste,

And a new society built on equality will last.

Their paths crossed at the University of Columbia,

Where Dewey was a professor and Ambedkar a fellow,

They spoke of democracy and its importance to all,

and of the struggles faced by those who were small.

Dewey saw the potential in Ambedkar's work,
And his ideas, he knew, could make society lurk,
Toward a new direction, a brighter future for all,
Ambedkar understood the worth of education,
In shattering chains of subjugation,
He sought Dewey's guidance, and they both put in work,
Toward a society where all could equally perk.

Their work continued, even when they were apart,
For Dewey, Ambedkar was a light in the dark,
A symbol of hope for a world in turmoil,
A voice of reason in a society that was spoiled.
For Ambedkar, Dewey was a mentor and guide,
whose ideas and values he would always abide,
A beacon of hope in a world so unjust,
A voice of reason in a society that was corrupt.

Dewey's influence on Ambedkar's work,
Is traced in his writings, speeches, and the way he'd walk,
Committed to equality, liberty, and fraternity,
Ambedkar found meaning in Buddhism's divinity.
Traditional materials and imagination,
used to see Buddhism's reconstruction,
Toward the meliorative ends of social reform,
Breaking the chains of caste, a norm.

Their work endures today in heart and mind,
Of those who strive to break down every wall,
Of oppression and discrimination's bind,
to build a world that's fair and just for all.
For Ambedkar and Dewey, their work was never done,
Their legacy lives on, and their ideas still run,
Through the veins of those who seek change,
And a better world for all to gain.

A Bridge Across The Chasms

In India's history,

Two leaders did collide,

Gandhi and Ambedkar

with sights quite a distinct inside,

One sought to unite the country,

Through nonviolence and love,

While the other battled against caste,

a structure from above.

The Poona Pact was a deal that they both signed,

In 1932, amidst great pressure and dissension,

It was a compromise that sought to unite.

to end a quarrel that had gone too deep for sight.

Ambedkar's mission was to
annihilate the caste and its power,
To deliver the depressed rights,
and a prospect to blossom.
Gandhi saw issues inversely.
a more ongoing approach he sought,
And to him, the caste's end,
through separation, could not be wrought.

But then came the Poona Pact,
a compromise to end the discord,
To ensure that the electorate
would not be divided by caste,
It granted reserved seats for the depressed,
but without separate electorates,
And thus, India moved one step closer.
towards a united fate.

Gandhi saw the Poona Pact as a victory,
a step forward for Dalits' rights,
But Ambedkar saw it as a loss.
a compromise that blurred the lines,
Their visions, though different,
brought change to the nation,
And their collaboration,
even in disagreement, was an inspiration.

Gandhi, a popular leader,
believed in the caste system's reform,
He sought to change it,
in a way that was peaceful and warm,
But Ambedkar, an untouchable,
saw the caste system's pain,
And he fought to abolish it,
for it to never reign.

Their paths were different.
but both sought changes.
To bring about a world,
which wasn't bound by social ranges.
Gandhi saw caste as
a means of social division,
While Ambedkar saw it,
as a form of social exclusion.

Gandhi aimed to reform Varna's way,
ending caste, but Varna still has to stay,
By uniting castes, he dreamed of a new India.
Through peaceful means, a future utopia.
But Ambedkar saw this as a mere extension.
Of the caste system, a continued pretension,
He believed in the abolition of the Varna system,
and the equality of all, as a new social wisdom.

Gandhi, a proponent of the caste system's reform,
saw the separate electorates as the wrong social norm,
He believed in unity and the need for a joint electorate,
But Ambedkar saw this as a mere form of murky debate.
Ambedkar, having seen the caste system's pain,
The discrimination and inequality, which it did retain.

Representation for oppressed, he believed,
Liberation through separate electorate could be achieved.
But Gandhi saw this as a threat to unity.
He did not see a division of society as a necessity.
He believed that joint electorates would ensure harmony.
and bring about change through peaceful diplomacy.
Disagreement of leaders, unrest it caused,
Difficult for Ambedkar, decision to pause.
He had to choose between separate or joint electorates,
And this decision would determine his people's fates.

After much deliberation, Ambedkar made his choice.
To accept the Pact and end the separate electorate's voice,
He did this out of a need for compromise.
and in the hope that eventually unity would arise.
But this decision left Ambedkar unhappy and unsatisfied.
As he felt that his people's rights were unjustifiably denied,
The pact wasn't enough to address the caste system's plight.
And it left Ambedkar in a state of social fight.

The Poona Pact did bring about some social reforms,
But it did not end the caste system's social norms.
Ambedkar continued to fight for his people's rights.
and bring about change—that was truly in sight.
The debate between these two great leaders,
highlighted the need for change in social pressures,
and led to the creation of the Constitution,
that sought to end the caste system's pollution.

The caste system still exists in many ways today.
But the work of these leaders has led the way.
To a more equal and just society, where all are free,
to live a life with dignity and opportunity.
In India, a land of diverse cultures and beliefs,
There are still divisions, which cause much grief.

The caste system, with a social hierarchy in place,
That keeps people down and limits their space.
At the heart of this system lies the Varna,
A classification of society that's been around for millennia,
The Brahmins, Kshatriyas, Vaishyas, and Shudras,
Untouchables were, always in history.
outside of this hierarchy,
considered impure and lower.

The Common Quest For Liberation

In the native land of a billion stories,

Where the crags soar high and the streams roll free,

been three men with a promise of liberation,

Ambedkar, Phule, and Periyar, makers of the nation.

Ambedkar, the offspring of an untouchable,

Phule, a harbinger of social justice,

Periyar, the song of the repressed,

They scrolled change for the depressed.

Ambedkar held Phule's teachings of humanity dear,

A message of equality to dispel caste's fear.

Through his words, he honoured Phule's legacy,

A tribute to a great teacher, for all, to see.

Together they fought against the oppressive reign,

Their voices echoing, they want to bring about change.

And though they're gone, their spirit lives on,

Inspiring generations to fight until dawn.

Ambedkar found in Phule's words,

A source of inspiration that spurred,

His fight for social justice and equality,

A bond that strengthened his resolve with quality.

Their connection went beyond words unsaid,

A shared vision for the depressed, both had,

And Ambedkar's journey was set in motion,

to follow Phule's lead with true devotion.

In a quest for social equality,

Ambedkar and Phule fought valiantly.

Their vision of a just society,

brought hope to those in poverty.

Ambedkar's Constitution gave legal power,

While Phule's education laid the foundation,

Together they paved the way,

toward a brighter and fairer day.

Periyar, the Tamil crusader,

He fought for justice, and his voice was a persuader.

With Ambedkar and Phule by his side,

Together, they challenged oppression, far and wide.

Their vision of equality and liberation,

Urges us to fight for a just nation.

Their legacy of social reform,

Calls for action to weather any storm.

Their message of freedom and liberation,

It shines brightly, like a beacon of inspiration.

Let us join hands and strive for a better way,

Where justice and equality are here to stay.

Ambedkar, Periyar, and Phule's vision,

A world where everyone has a decision.

Let us rise and make their dream come true,

a world where freedom and liberation are for me and you.

Ideological Differences Yet Unite

In India's land, two leaders held their places,

Ambedkar and Nehru remembered with grace,

With fervour and foresight, they both did aspire,

To forge a nation, just and ablaze with fire.

Ambedkar fought against the chains of caste,

And with a pen, he freed the depressed at last,

While Nehru sought to build a land of peace,

where all could live and flourish with great ease.

Ambedkar, a fighter for the Dalits' rights,

For the marginalized, he took up their fights,

Nehru's vision of progress and peace,

to build a nation where all would find release.

Yet, amidst their shared vision, there arose a disagreement,

On the paths, they held divergent sentiments,

For Ambedkar, the issue of caste discrimination,

was one that required immediate and radical eradication.

He fought for the rights of marginalized castes,

and proposed a separate electorate, in different ways.

Nehru had a different view of the whole nation,

Sought to unite, with no division persuasion.

A separate electorate could cause subdivision,

Nehru opposed it and saw it as a threat to the nation.

Their differences show how to reach a goal,

With different ways to make a nation whole.

They differed in their visions of a new India's creation,

Ambedkar sought to change with a depressed' inspiration,

Ambedkar's caste struggle fuelled his vision,

While Nehru aimed for a unified nation's mission.

Their differing backgrounds caused a rift,

As they debated their respective gifts.

Nehru sought a sustainable frame,

For progress and development with balanced aim.

Their heated conversation arose from varied views,

A complex issue that both had to muse.

In a land of democracy and debate,

Disagreements arose, but they didn't hate,

Ambedkar and Nehru, with their priorities, aligned,

The nation's progress was always on their minds.

Their views may differ, but their arguments were true,

A free, fair, and just nation was their virtue.

With dialogue and debate, they found a way,

To resolve their issues and for the nation, they'd stay.

Ambedkar and Nehru, two students of western history,

Their disagreements are a testament to a vibrant democracy,

In a democracy, ideas can clash and collide,

Yet, it is the people's wish that will always decide.

Visionaries' Allies For Breaking Shackles

Ambedkar and Shahu Ji Maharaj, two great men of our land,

Both born into lower castes with a desire to take a stand,

Against the oppressive caste system, which held them down,

And to empower their people with education and renown.

Shahu Ji Maharaj, the ruler of the Kolhapur state,

Was a visionary and reformer who believed in fate,

Every individual, regardless of caste and creed,

Had a right to education and the tools they needed.

Ambedkar, a brilliant scholar with a thirst for knowledge,

Shared Shahu's vision and fought against the bondage,

Of the caste system, which restricted and depressed,

And sought to elevate the subjugated with every breath.

Shahu Ji worked to establish schools and colleges,

To educate the masses' and break the caste entrenchments,

Shahu Ji established hostels and scholarships for the poor,

to ensure that every person had an equal door.

Ambedkar and Shahu, a powerful team,

Who fought for the suppressed dream,

To create a just and equitable society,

free   the chains of caste and patriarchy.

We remember Ambedkar and Shahu Ji Maharaj,

Two great men, who fought for a cause without a flaw,

They knew that education was the key,

To liberate their people and to set them free.

Struggle Beyond The Oceans

Ambedkar's struggle was not just for his land,

It was for a world that must understand,

That oppression takes many forms,

and that justice must be uniform.

Du Bois, a leader in his own right,

fought for justice with all his might,

For black Americans, who were oppressed,

for a world that was callous and didn't give them rest.

A race, as Du Bois has proclaimed,

is but binding of humans to blame,

Forced to share blood, language, and the past,

Struggling together, their ideals to amass

Voluntarily and involuntarily, they toil,

For goals that are vividly but painfully boiled,

Their traditions and impulses are stifling their lives,

a community of purpose imposed by knives.

This definition, a facade of diversity,

Only serves to masquerade our true adversity,

Because it erases individual experiences,

and crushes our search for unique identities.

Let us not celebrate these imposed bonds.

For they are but chains that keep us from absconding.

From a race that is not biological but social,

built on hierarchies that are simply brutal.

For Ambedkar, caste was the enemy.

Of justice, of the world that would be,

Caste is an artificial partition,

Driven by endogamy, a custom of tradition,

maintaining division with no fusion,

and by doing so, perpetuating social discrimination.

Endogamy is the custom; that's to blame.

Preventing the fusion of different castes,

Thus, by giving each one a unique name,

A rigid hierarchy, that forever lasts.

The superposition of endogamy,

On exogamy, which leads to creation,

Caste, with its societal stratigraphy,

a system built on the foundation of separation.

But for both leaders, the fight was the same.

To end oppression and end the brutal game,

Of a system that rebuffed people their rights,

to live in a world that is just and bright.

For Ambedkar and Du Bois, race and caste

Were the barriers that wouldn't last,

They saw the need for a new social order,

Where oppression wouldn't border,

In the lives of those who were oppressed,

on the lives of those who were stressed.

Ambedkar and Du Bois saw the link,

Between race and caste and the need to think,

About a world that was free from both,

a world that would give everyone growth.

In the land of India and the US,

Their legacy lives on without a fuss.

Their fight for justice is not just for one,

It's for everyone, for every daughter and son.

Ambedkar and Du Bois fought for us all.

For a world that's free, where oppression will fall,

And that is the legacy they left behind.

for a world that's just and kind.

Triumphs Of Three: Education, Peace, And Division

In the spheres of politics and history,

There were many who left their legacies.

Their views and ideas often conflicted,

But their passion for change never wavered.

Amongst them were Ambedkar and Ranade,

Two crusaders who refused to fade.

Both fought for social justice and human rights,

and aimed to end India's caste divisions.

The Deccan Sabha of Poona invited Ambedkar to speak,

On the 101st birthday of Justice Ranade, so meek,

Ambedkar knew his opinions would not please,

But in the end, he accepted the invitation with ease.

As Ambedkar had no intention to publish his discourse,

Speeches on anniversaries are not of many courses,

But his troublesome friends insisted on it being seen,

And though indifferent, he did not want to be mean.

So let his discourse on this great man be seen,
And let his legacy live on forever, evergreen,
For Justice Ranade, who was a beacon of justice and equality,
a true inspiration for all humanity.
"Politics," once noble, is now a game of the show,
A challenge of extravagance, a spectacle to behold,
Gandhi and Jinnah, two popular men of old,
Competing constantly, with no end in sight, so.

Gandhi, the Mahatma, was esteemed and idolised.
Jinnah, the "Quaid E Azam," equally grand,
Congress and the Muslim League, in their hands,
Working committees and councils, more and more.
Ambedkar was no worshipper of symbols,
He believes in smashing them down.
If he dislikes Gandhi and Jinnah,
It's because he loves India's ground.

The true commitment of a nationalist,
is to see the country beyond the men,
To worship Gandhi or Jinnah,
undermines the service that drives them.
Ambedkar expects that his countrymen,
will learn to separate the two,
That India's greatness lies beyond,
The idols they blindly pursue.

Gandhi, too, had his sight on change,

Through non-violence, he aimed to rearrange.

He also talked about a future without discrimination,

and surely fought for India's liberation.

Jinnah, on the other hand, had his plan,

to create an independent Muslim homeland.

He foresaw a nation built on religion,

And fought for his people's identification.

These figures, with their diverse views,

Show us how ideas can both unite and confuse.

Though their paths were different in scope,

All aimed to create a more just world and cope.

Ambedkar and Ranade's paths were intertwined,

Both fought against caste with a fervent mind.

Their vision for an equitable society,

Lives on today with great piety.

Ranade, with his faith in education,
saw the pathway to a better nation.
He knew that with knowledge came power,
and intended to give it to every flower.
Gandhi, with his way of peace,
Battled for Indian independence with ease.

He indicated to the world that change could come,
through peaceful means, and not just a gun.
Jinnah, with his aim of a separate land,
had a vision that not all could understand.
Though divisive, his work was strong,
And headed to a nation that still stands long.

The Trail Continues

Ambedkar, a visionary, was ahead of his time,

A leader who fought for a world that's sublime.

His relevance, even today, is clear,

His vision is a guiding light to which all should adhere.

He fought for the depressed, for their rights and their voice,

He challenged the status quo and gave us a choice.

He saw a world where every person was free,

and fought for justice relentlessly with great glee.

In today's India, his relevance is more important than ever,

As we grapple with issues that we cannot sever.

Inequality, injustice, and discrimination still prevail,

And Ambedkar's vision can help us set sail.

Ambedkar's relevance isn't just in our nation,

His vision is for a world in need of liberation.

He fought for the rights of the poor, weak, and women,

Showing freedom's is a mountain to climb in.

He saw a world where all could gain an education,
and where every child had equal opportunity in every nation.
He knew that knowledge unlocks potential, is truly great,
His belief was exceptional; there was no debate.
His vision spanned beyond the present time,
a future where every person's voice would chime.
He saw a world where the depressed had a say,
not brushed aside but uplifted in every way.

Ambedkar's relevance goes beyond his time,
His vision can guide us, in this era of clime.
He knew change wouldn't come without a fight,
and believed in our collective power to do what's right.
Ambedkar's vision is not just a dream so far,
We can make it real, brick by brick, star by star.
Inspired by his life and work, let's take a cue,
His vision to guide us is always strong and true.

Ambedkar's vision of justice and equality,
not limited to his lifetime or nationality.
He believed in a future where every human being,
Living with dignity, respect, and meaning to glean.
He fought against caste and discrimination's sway,
Worked tirelessly for social and economic Freedom Day.
He recognized the power of education as a tool,
to break the chains of ignorance and ignorance's rule.

Discrimination lingers on in caste, race, and gender,
Ambedkar's message reminds us of the need to be tender.
He fought for women's rights and their deserving place,
Gender equality is his vision, must embraced with grace.
Ambedkar's call for equality in social and economic space,
relevant now as we face the world's complexity and pace.
The gap between the rich and the poor widens every day,
Ambedkar reminds us to realign and find a better way.

Ambedkar didn't reject equality, but communism's brutality,
He believed in an inclusive, just democracy, not partiality.
Every voice heard, with respect and trust,
That was Ambedkar's vision: dignity for all was a must.
Ambedkar's message was not just for his nation,
But for all the world, every human creation.
Compassion, empathy, and humanity are his calls.
It is for the world's sanity, for the well-being of all.

In a world that still grapples with inequality and injustice,
Ambedkar's vision is an abiding practice.
Universal brotherhood, dignity for every soul,
Still relevant and vital today, we must answer his call.
Let's build the world Ambedkar dreamt of every being,
End oppression's reign; strive towards equality's freeing.
His message is a guiding lesson: for justice, we must strive,
Remembering his vision, in every step we take, we thrive.

Methodology

Ambedkar, with intellect sharp,
Reformed history, with a critical harp.
Ambedkar's historiography broke the mould,
His insights and critiques are always so bold.
Sociology, philosophy, a mind so brilliant,
His legacy shines with historical might.

Ambedkar's methodology of social sciences,
A rigorous approach with no pretences.
Empirical evidence, reason, and analysis,
His framework, a path to social justice.
In studying society, he used a critical lens,
Examining power, oppression, and trends.
His focus on the marginalized and depressed,
a methodology that truly impressed.

His methodology of social sciences, a tool to transform,
society, with equality and justice as the norm.
Ambedkar's methodology was rooted in reality,
drawing from experience, not just ideology.
He emphasized the importance of data and facts,
to uncover truths and counteract false acts.

Ambedkar's economic methodology, bold and new,
Embracing state intervention for social progress to ensue.
His focus was on land reforms and industrialization,
a path to economic growth and modernization.
Rejecting laissez-faire, his ideas were ahead of their time,
A visionary approach that still resonates in our paradigm.
Ambedkar believed that economics should serve,
the needs of the people, not just those with the nerve.
His methodology emphasized distributive justice,
To address poverty and inequality, this is a must.

Ambedkar's criticism of colonialism was fierce,
exposing the injustice and exploitation without fear.
He denounced the "divide and rule" policy of the British,
Their attempts and his condemnation never ended.
He saw through their civilizing mission façade,
With their suppression to India's progress, his anger clawed.
Ambedkar's critique of colonialism was a call to action,
to resist oppression and strive for liberation.

Ambedkar's methodology of religion was unique,
Approaching both with a critical and rational technique.
He believed in the importance of questioning beliefs,
And rejected blind faith to counteract societal grief.
His methodology emphasized a scientific temper,
To challenge superstitions and beliefs that hamper
The progress of society and perpetuating inequality,
A call for rationalism to achieve true liberty.
Ambedkar's wisdom as an academic was profound,
Emphasizing the value of knowledge, which knows no
bounds.

Tribute

Ambedkar's trail inspires my pen to write,
His unwavering spirit, his quest for rights,
Learning without compromise, day and night,
dreaming of Columbia's intellectual might.
How do I admire you? Let me reflect,
Your passion, your knowledge, your intellect,
Your struggles resonate and connect.

A personality that loiters, an eternal prospect.
Let me compare you to a prune so sweet,
Your brilliance and grit, always on beat,
Precise, focused, and with a purpose to meet.
As I depart, my heart and soul are astir,
The world shall recall my words with a loud blur,
while you, Ambedkar, remain an eternal star.

Bibliography

Abhinav. "W. E. B. Du Bois and Ambedkar: Revisiting the intellectual historical analysis of their views on race and caste." *Social Science Journal for Advanced Research* 3, no. 1 (2023). 25-32. https://ssrn.com/abstract=4368120

Ambedkar, B. R. *Dr. Babasaheb Ambedkar: Writings and Speeches, vols 1–17*. Mumbai: Education Department of the Government of Maharashtra. 2014. https://doj.gov.in/dr-b-r-ambedkar/

Ambedkar, Bhimrao Ramji. *Dr. Ambedkar and Democracy: An Anthology*. Oxford University Press, 2018.

Ambedkar, Bhimrao Ramji. *Riddles in Hinduism: An Exposition to Enlighten the Masses: the Annotated Critical Selection*. Navayana, 2016.

Ambedkar, Bhimrao Ramji. *The Buddha and his dhamma: A critical edition*. Oxford University Press, 2011.

Ambedkar, Savita. *Babasaheb: My Life With Dr Ambedkar*. India: Penguin, 2022.

Ashwajith, Milind, and Sreejith Rajni. "Philosophy of Education-Ambedkar, Savitribai Phule, Jotiba Phule."

Banningan, John A. "The Hindu code bill." *Far Eastern Survey* 21, no. 17 (1952): 173-176.

Bardia, Meena. "Dr. BR Ambedkar his ideas about religion and conversion to Buddhism." *The Indian Journal of Political Science* (2009): 737-749.

Campion, Sonali. "Educate, agitate, organise: a short biography of Dr BR Ambedkar." *South Asia@ LSE* (2016).

Cháirez-Garza, Jesús Francisco. "BR Ambedkar, Franz Boas and the rejection of racial theories of untouchability." *South Asia: Journal of South Asian Studies* 41, no. 2 (2018): 281-296.

Chakravarti, Uma, and M. Mohanty. "Conceptualizing Brahmanical patriarchy in early India: Gender, caste, class and state." *New Delhi: Sage Publications* (2004).

Chaudhary, Poonam. "Hindu Code Bill: Towards Liberation of Women." *Contemporary Voice of Dalit* 8, no. 2 (2016): 153-162.

Deshpande, G. P. "Marx and Ambedkar: some unacademic reflections." (1987): 1862-1864.

Dhara, Lalitha. "Ambedkar's understated feminism." *AMBEDKAR* (2022): 143.

Doctor, Adi H. "Low caste protest movements in 19th and 20th century Maharashtra: A study of Jotirao Phule and BR Ambedkar." (1991).

Fitzgerald, Timothy. "From structure to substance: Ambedkar, Dumont and orientalism." *Contributions to Indian sociology* 30, no. 2 (1996): 273-288.

Gandhi, Rajmohan. "Independence and Social Justice: The Ambedkar–Gandhi Debate." *Economic and Political Weekly* (2015): 35-44.

Gandhi, Rajmohan. "Response to Arundhati Roy." *Economic and Political Weekly* (2015): 83-85.

Ghosal, Debjani. "BR Ambedkar: The Messiah and Emancipator of Indian Women." *Contemporary Voice of Dalit* (2022): 2455328X211067113.

Gokhale, Balkrishna Govind. "Dr. Bhimrao Ramji Ambedkar: Rebel against Hindu Tradition." In *Religion and Social Conflict in South Asia*, pp. 13-23. Brill, 1976.

Goyal, Kaushal. *B. R. Ambedkar: A Biography*. Pigeon Books, 2016.

Granville, Austin. The Indian Constitution: Cornerstone of Nation. Oxford University Press, 1966.

Guru, Gopal. "Appropriating Ambedkar." *Economic and Political Weekly* (1991): 1697-1699.

Halli, Chandrakala S., and Shridhar M. Mullal. "Dr. BR Ambedkar and Hindu Code Bill, women measure legislation." *Imperial Journal of Interdisciplinary Research (IJIR)* 2, no. 3 (2016): 7-10.

Jaffrelot, Christophe. *Dr Ambedkar and untouchability: analysing and fighting caste*. Orient Blackswan, 2006.

Kadankavil, Thomas. "Religion and politics: Interpretations of Gandhi, Nehru and Ambedkar." *Journal of Dharma* 25, no. 3&4 (2000): 345-368.

Kapoor, S. D. "BR Ambedkar, WEB DuBois and the process of liberation." *Economic and Political Weekly* (2003): 5344-5349.

Keer, Dhananjay. *Dr. Ambedkar: life and mission*. Popular Prakashan, 1995.

Keer, Dhananjay. *Mahatma Jotirao Phooley: father of the Indian social revolution*. Popular Prakashan, 1997.

Kumar, Ravinder. "Gandhi, Ambedkar and the Poona pact, 1932." *South Asia: Journal of South Asian Studies* 8, no. 1-2 (1985): 87-101.

Kumar, Sanjeev. "Ambedkar's journey of conversion to Buddhism." *Contemporary voice of Dalit* 11, no. 2 (2019): 107-118.

Mahesh, Mr, and Anil Kumar Thakur. "Social Justice in India and Contribution of Various People in the Upliftment of Dalits." *Int. J. of Multidisciplinary and Current research* 3 (2015).

Mallik, Basanta Kumar. "Jyotirao Govindrao Phule." In *Revisiting Modern Indian Thought*, pp. 57-72. Routledge India, 2021.

Manoharan, Karthick Ram. "In the path of Ambedkar: Periyar and the Dalit question." *South Asian History and Culture* 11, no. 2 (2020): 136-149.

Nadkarni, M. V. *Handbook of Hinduism*. New Delhi: Ane Books Pvt. Ltd, 2013.

Omvedt, Gail. "" Patriarchy:" the Analysis of Women's Oppression." *Insurgent Sociologist* 13, no. 3 (1986): 30-50.

Omvedt, Gail. "Jotirao Phule and the ideology of social revolution in India." *Economic and political weekly* (1971): 1969-1979.

Omvedt, Gail. *Ambedkar: towards an enlightened India*. Penguin UK, 2017.

Omvedt, Gail. *Buddhism in India: challenging Brahmanism and caste*. Sage Publications India, 2003.

Omvedt, Gail. *Dalits and the democratic revolution: Dr Ambedkar and the Dalit movement in colonial India*. SAGE Publications India, 1994.

Paul, Satyaki, and Sabatini Chatterjee. "Babasaheb Dr. Ambedkar and his role in Nation-Building for Modern India." *IJFMR-International Journal For Multidisciplinary Research* 4, no. 6 (2022).

Rege, Sharmila. "Ramabai and Ambedkar 1." In *Dalit Feminist Theory*, pp. 94-100. Routledge India, 2019.

Rose, Gladin, and Janaky Sreedharan. "Brahmanical patriarchy: A paradigm of patriarchal power." *Research Journal of English Language and Literature* 3, no. 2 (2015): 190-196.

Roy, Arundhati. *The doctor and the saint: Caste, race, and annihilation of caste: The debate between BR Ambedkar and MK Gandhi*. Haymarket Books+ ORM, 2017.

Sampath, Rajesh. "A commentary on Ambedkar's posthumously published "Philosophy of Hinduism"." *CASTE: A Global Journal on Social Exclusion* 1, no. 1 (2020): 17-28.

Sampath, Rajesh. "A Commentary on Ambedkar's Posthumously Published Philosophy of Hinduism–Part II." *CASTE: A Global Journal on Social Exclusion* 2, no. 1 (2021): 1-16.

Sampath, Rajesh. "A Commentary on Ambedkar's Posthumously Published "Philosophy of Hinduism"–Part III." *CASTE: A Global Journal on Social Exclusion* 2, no. 2 (2021): 219-234.

Singariya, M. R. "Dr. BR Ambedkar and women empowerment in India." *Quest Journals Journal of Research in Humanities and Social Science* 2, no. 1 (2014): 1-4.

Singh, Asha. "The Periyar Project." https://theperiyarproject.com/

Tharoor, Shashi. *Ambedkar: A life*. Aleph Book Company, 2022.

Vajpeyi, Ananya. "Ambedkar and the Struggle for Women's Equality." *Antyajaa: Indian Journal of Women and Social Change* 1, no. 1 (2016): 5-9.

Williams, Rina Verma. "Hindu law as personal law: state and identity in the Hindu Code Bill Debates, 1952–1956." *See Lubin et al* (2010): 105-20.

Figure 1 Chavdar Tale Satyagrah at Mahad (25th December 1927), Source: https://www.symbiosis-ambedkarmemorial.org/oldphotographs.php

Figure 2 Kalaram Mandir Satyagrah, Source: https://www.symbiosis-ambedkarmemorial.org/oldphotographs.php

Figure 3 Dr.Babasaheb's Family Circle, Source: https://www.symbiosis-ambedkarmemorial.org/oldphotographs.php

Figure 4 Dr.Ambedkar is standing in Grief near dead body of his wife Smt. Ramabai Ambedkar, Source: https://www.symbiosis-ambedkarmemorial.org/oldphotographs.php

Figure 5 Dr. Babasaheb in his Library, Source: https://www.symbiosis-ambedkarmemorial.org/oldphotographs.php

Figure 6 The Constitution Committee (29th August 1947), Source: https://www.symbiosis-ambedkarmemorial.org/oldphotographs.php

Figure 7 Submission of the draft of the Indian Constitution (February 1948), Source: https://www.symbiosis-ambedkarmemorial.org/oldphotographs.php

Figure 8 Dr. Babasaheb Ambedkar taking the oath, Source: https://www.symbiosis-ambedkarmemorial.org/oldphotographs.php

Figure 9 Embraced Buddhism at Nagpur (14th October 1956), Source:
https://www.symbiosis-ambedkarmemorial.org/oldphotographs.php

Figure 10 Bharatratna - Dr. Ambedkar (14th April 1990), Source:
https://www.symbiosis-ambedkarmemorial.org/oldphotographs.php